Everything You Need To Know About

SEXUAL ABUSE

Boys and girls should be told how to protect themselves from sexual abuse.

Everything You Need To Know About
SEXUAL ABUSE

Evan Stark, Ph.D.

and

Marsha Holly, Ph.D.

THE ROSEN PUBLISHING GROUP, INC.
NEW YORK

Published in 1988, 1991 by The Rosen Publishing Group, Inc.
29 East 21st Street, New York City, New York 10010

Revised Edition 1991
Copyright 1988, 1991 by The Rosen Publishing Group, Inc.

Manufactured in the United States of America

Library of Congress Cataloging-in-Publication Data

Stark, Evan.
    Everything you need to know about sexual abuse / Evan Stark and
Marsha Holly.
    (The Need to know library)
    Bibliography: p. 62
    Includes index.
    Summary: Identifies forms of sexual abuse and offers advice on how
to get help and how to avoid such abuse.
    ISBN 0-8239-1245-0
    1. Child molesting—Juvenile   literature. 2. Incest—Juvenile
literature. [1. Child molesting. 2. Incest. 3. Child abuse.]
I. Holly, Marsha. II. Title. III. Series.
HQ71.S72 1988
362.7'044—dc19
                                    88-18114
                                        CIP
                                        AC

Contents

Introduction

Everyone likes to be hugged or touched by someone they care for. But there are some kinds of touching that are not good. When someone hugs you so hard it really hurts, that is abuse.

Getting a kiss on your face or mouth can feel good. But a kiss can feel bad when it comes from someone you don't like or someone you don't know or when it lasts too long. This is another example of abuse. This book will help you recognize one type of abuse—sexual abuse—and help you know what to do about it.

Sexual abuse occurs when an older person forces a child to do sexual things. The older person is stronger than the child. So sexual abuse can involve physical force. Children may also do something sexual with an older person because they have learned to trust and obey adults. Or an adult may promise you something you really want. These types of sexual abuse hurt as much as physical harm.

Everyone finds it unpleasant to imagine a child being forced into sexual activities. But by being

All children like to be touched by someone they love and trust.

informed about sexual abuse, you may be able to help yourself, a friend, or a family member who has this problem.

Remember this. Stopping sexual abuse is not your responsibility. It is the job of adults. But adults can only stop sexual abuse when they know about it.

Some things in this book may have happened to you or to a person you know. If so, talk it over with an adult who will listen.

7

An invitation may not feel right. It's best to say "no."

Chapter 1

Saying No

Two Stories

You are waiting for the school bus with some friends. A car pulls up. A man leans out, smiles, and calls you over. He asks where the nearest Happy Burger is. You tell him.

"Do you want to come along?" he asks.

You'd love to go to Happy Burger. But you say no. When he leaves, you and your friends talk about it. They agree you did the right thing. "He was weird," a friend says.

The rules about strangers are clear. If the man got out of the car and tried to grab you, you would be scared. But you would know what to say and do. You would tell the man to get lost. You might scream, call for help, kick him, pull away, or run. When you got home, you would tell your parents. They might call the police.

Now let's change the story.

This time, you know the man in the car. He's the coach from your school.

"Do you want a ride?" the coach asks.

You're not sure what to do. Your friends are watching. You feel funny. But you don't want to be rude.

"Go ahead," says a friend. You get in the car.

On the way home he stops at Happy Burger. He gets you a Coke and a burger, to go. As you're leaving, he pats your backside. You feel funny again. Is something wrong?

When you return to the car, he puts his arm around you. His arm feels safe. But you pull away. He takes his arm away. Then he puts his hand on your leg. He stops at the edge of the park. He asks if you feel lonely. While you talk, he rubs your leg. He rubs your leg in a way that makes you feel uncomfortable.

He takes you to your house. "See you," he says.

Later, your mother asks about your day. You tell her about the ride home. But you don't tell her that the coach rubbed your leg and patted your backside. You act so strange that she asks what's wrong. After dinner, you cry. Then you tell her what happened. Talking makes you feel better.

When you were young, you were warned about strangers who try to grab or hurt young people. Those persons are called *molesters*. Molesters are almost always men. And they are usually strangers.

But did you know that people your age are much more likely to be hurt or bothered sexually by a person they know well, like the coach? It could be a scout leader, a neighbor, a doctor, a teacher, a minister, or the father of a friend. Or it could be a member of your own family, like your brother, father, or stepfather. The family members who most often abuse children are fathers and brothers. Sometimes even mothers abuse their children.

We are taught to respect and obey older persons. The hardest thing about sexual abuse is that the abuser is usually someone you trust. It may be someone who is responsible for taking care of you. It may be someone you love. It is almost always someone you want to care about you. The problem is that you may not know how to act or what to say when this happens.

Do you have the right to ask your big brother or sister to knock on the bedroom door before they enter the room?

Can you tell your mom or dad they can't come in the bathroom if you don't want them there?

What happens if your babysitter says "I will let you stay up late and watch a video if you play a game with me and take off your clothes?"

The first step in dealing with sexual abuse is learning how to say no. The problem is that saying no to an adult or someone you trust is not always easy. That's why you have this book.

Teachers and parents help youngsters by listening and talking about sexual abuse.

Chapter 2

The Secret That Is Being Shared

This chapter answers questions that are often asked about sexual abuse.

When we call abuse "sexual," what do we mean?

"Sexual" means the parts of your body that can give you great pleasure when you are in love. The main sexual parts of the body are a girl's vagina and a boy's penis. These body organs are used in reproduction and are called *genitals*. In the story, the coach rubbed the young person's leg in a sexual way. Other parts of your body such as your breasts, your backside, or your mouth can also be sexual.

Sexual abuse means using a child for sexual pleasure. Sexual abuse is a crime.

Sexual abuse usually happens only on the sexual parts of the body. Many dads have kissed a little girl's toes, fingertips, knees, tummy, and backside. But when those kisses or rubs are *only* on the tummy, backside, or chest—even if they aren't on the genitals—they probably are bad.

The abuser may touch a young person's sexual parts. The abuser may want the child to touch him (or her) sexually. Or the abuser may use the young person in some other way for sexual activity.

A male may put his penis into a girl's vagina. This is called *intercourse*. A female abuser may force a young boy to have intercourse. When a child has intercourse with a parent, a brother, or a sister, the abuse is called *incest*. Pregnancy is one danger when abuse includes intercourse.

Does sexual abuse happen to boys or girls?

What do you think? Was the child in the two stories a boy or a girl?

You probably said girl. Girls are more likely to be abused than boys. The child in the story could also have been a boy. Boys are also sexually abused. Whether the victim is a boy or a girl, most sexual abuse is committed by men. But mothers also commit sexual abuse.

How common is sexual abuse?

Sexual abuse is far more common than most people think. So is incest.

Count the girls and boys in your class. Do you think any children in your class had an experience like the child in the story? Some probably have. One of every four girls and one of every seven boys may be sexually abused before they reach eighteen.

Does sexual abuse always involve force?

Many abusers use force. Others use threats. The abuser may threaten to hurt the child or someone the child loves, like her mother. Or a parent may threaten to go away and never come back if the child tells what happened. Or he may say that the child will be taken away if anyone learns about the abuse.

But sexual abuse does not always involve force or threats. Many abusers use bribes or presents to get the child to do what they want. They promise something special, like money or new clothes.

Often sexual abuse starts with a game, like tickling or grabbing or make-believe. The abuser wants the child to trust him. Then, one day, the game becomes sexual.

Sexual abuse is wrong even when no force is involved.

Does sexual abuse always hurt?

Sexual abuse can cause serious problems even when there is no violence or intercourse. Children who are abused feel isolated from other children. They may feel ashamed about what has happened.

They may think they are not worth much. Those
feelings are called low self-esteem. They may feel
so angry that they hurt another child, or a pet. Or
they may try to hurt themselves. Some children
who are sexually abused become very sad or
withdrawn. This is called depression.

Sexual abuse can also cause problems when a
child becomes an adult. Adults who were sexually
abused often don't trust others. Or they may want
to avoid sex altogether.

The longer sexual abuse goes on, the more
damage it can cause.

Not all children who are sexually abused suffer
long-term effects. If the abuse is stopped early and
the child finds someone they trust to talk to, many
of the harmful effects of sexual abuse can be
prevented.

What causes sexual abuse?

A myth is something most people believe that is
not true. One myth is that sexual abusers are sick.
Another myth is that sexual abuse only happens in
families that have a lot of other problems as well.

Some abusers have serious mental health
problems. Some are sexually attracted to children,
but not to other adults. And some abusers were
sexually or physically abused themselves when they
were children. Some families where sexual abuse
occurs also have other problems. The husband may
be beating his wife. The mother may be disabled.

Finding a friend to talk to can help stop abuse.

But most sexual abuse occurs in ordinary families and is committed by ordinary men.

The abuser wants things his own way. He likes being in control and having power over others. This is why he is attracted to someone who is smaller and weaker than he is, like a child.

How old are children who are sexually abused?

Children are most in danger of being sexually abused when they are between nine and twelve years old. But the child may be two, or even seventeen.

How have we learned so much about sexual abuse?

We learn about sexual abuse when people who have been sexually abused tell their stories.

Adults who were hurt by sexual abuse as children are talking about it. Children are talking too. They are telling their stories to teachers, nurses, parents, and friends—to anyone who will listen.

Parents, doctors, teachers, police, and others who want to help and protect children are learning about sexual abuse.

Sexual abuse is on TV and the radio and in the newspapers. Young people all over are speaking out. Sexual abuse is the secret that is now being shared.

Chapter 3

The Seven Rules

The stories in this book come from girls and boys who got help. The boys and girls use seven rules to solve their problems. These rules can help you understand and respond to sexual abuse.

Rule #1. <u>YOUR BODY BELONGS TO YOU.</u>
You, and only you, should decide how to use your body sexually. In sexual abuse, someone who is older and more powerful decides how to use your body. This is wrong. You have a right to say no.

Rule #2. <u>SEXUAL ABUSE IS NEVER YOUR</u>
<u>FAULT.</u>
Children are not responsible for what adults or other older persons do. Abuse is not their fault, even if they cannot say no or if they enjoy the attention they get from the abuser. Nothing a child does, or doesn't do, excuses an older person who uses a child for sexual pleasure.

Some men attend counseling sessions to discuss their problems as abusers.

Rule #3. SEXUAL ABUSE IS ALWAYS
   HARMFUL.

Sexual abuse always hurts the child. Sometimes the child's body is hurt. If a girl who is old enough to have babies is abused, she can get pregnant. But the deepest hurt is the way sexual abuse makes children feel. Sexual abuse always makes children feel bad about themselves. These feelings can make it hard to work in school, to have friends, or to have fun.

Rule #4. GOOD PEOPLE DO BAD THINGS.

It is hard to believe that someone we love or who is kind to us can sexually abuse us. Abusers may be good persons in other ways. They may give presents. Or they may be gentle when they want sex. But the abuse is very, very wrong and must be stopped.

Rule #5. SEXUAL ABUSE DOES NOT STOP
   BY ITSELF.

Sexual abuse is hard to talk about. Children are sometimes afraid of the abuser. But sexual abuse usually goes on until the abuser is made to stop. The best way to stop sexual abuse is to tell an adult who will listen and do something about it.

There are special people, child workers, whose job is to protect children from abuse. Adults know how to find these people.

Sexual abuse always hurts. It creates feelings of shame and loneliness.

Rule #6. KEEP TELLING PEOPLE YOU
    TRUST ABOUT SEXUAL ABUSE UNTIL
    SOMEONE LISTENS.

Some adults may not believe a child. Other
adults may tell the young person to forget about
the problem. But remember, sexual abuse does not
stop by itself. If one adult doesn't do the right
thing, tell another who will.

Rule #7. WHAT HAPPENS TO A SEXUAL
    ABUSER IS NEVER YOUR FAULT.

Children feel, "If I tell, then what happens to
the abuser is my fault." Because sexual abuse is a
crime, some abusers go to jail. Others leave the
house. When the abuser is someone you care
about, this is very hard. Some abusers stop when
they are told it is wrong. Some abusers need to see
a doctor. Remember, only the sexual abuser is
responsible for what happens when abuse is
uncovered.

The next few chapters tell the stories of children
who said no to abuse. See if the Seven Rules help
you understand what happened to them—and what
they did *to help themselves*.

Chapter 4

Your Body Belongs To You

Debra lives in a house with her mom, her dad, her grandfather and her dog. After her eleventh birthday party, she looked at herself in the mirror. She noticed that her breasts were beginning to form. She looked at the rest of her body and felt good about it.

Suddenly, her grandfather walked into the room. He laughed at her in front of the mirror. He made fun of her body.

"I suppose you think you need a bra," he teased.

Debra felt hurt. She had wondered if she could wear a bra. Some of her friends wore them already. But what her grandfather said made her feel ashamed. When he made fun of her, she thought she was no good.

A few weeks later, her grandfather walked into the bathroom while Debra was taking a bath. At first

A father should respect his daughter's privacy.

she thought it was a mistake. But he wouldn't leave when she asked him. She wrapped a towel around herself. But he yanked it off. Then he grabbed her from behind. He held her breasts.

"Cut it out," she yelled. She tried to get free.

"You used to like being tickled," he said.

"I'm not a little girl anymore," Debra said. She got really angry. She felt dirty and wanted to die. He told her not to tell her parents or he would have to leave the house.

She didn't want her grandfather to go. Although he kept bothering her, she decided not to tell her mom and dad.

Debra is growing up. Her body is changing. She feels bashful because she is not always sure what's happening. She needs time to get used to her body. It's really a new body all the time. Debra needs privacy to explore herself and learn about her body. She has a right to privacy. Some day she will want someone her own age to touch her breasts. And that's okay.

Her grandfather has no respect for Debra. He wants to see her naked. He pretends he's kidding. But abuse is no joke.

What Debra Did

One day, Mrs. Markle, a teacher at Debra's school, saw her crying in the girl's bathroom. Debra told Mrs. Markle why she was so upset. Mrs. Markle questioned Debra closely. Then she told

Debra she had done the right thing to tell her. She explained that there was no reason for Debra to hate herself. The feelings she has about herself come from her grandfather's abuse.

Mrs. Markle called a social worker at the child protection office and the social worker came to the house. She explained that Debra's grandpa would have to live somewhere else.

When Debra got home, her mother was angry. "Why didn't you just tell me what happened?" she yelled.

"I didn't think you would believe me," Debra said. "And grandpa told me not to tell or he would have to leave the house."

"I don't want grandpa to go either but he'll have to." her mother said. "I'm really upset you didn't tell me. I would have stopped him."

The most important lesson Debra learned was Rule #1, Your Body Belongs to You.

It's *your* body. You have a right to have your body respected, comforted, and loved only in ways that please you or that benefit you.

Rule #2, Abuse Is Never Your Fault.

Debra was confused about what happened. (When she was little, she liked to be held by her grandfather. Even now, she likes him to give her a goodnight kiss.) She wondered if she did something wrong.

Finding someone who will listen is the first step toward ending abuse.

Nothing Debra did was wrong. Children are not responsible for the sexual behavior of adults.

Rule #3, Abuse Always Hurts.
Debra's grandfather made her feel her body was no good. Even though he didn't hurt her physically, after he grabbed her breasts, she hurt so much inside, she wanted to die or run away. She cried.

Rule #4, Good People Do Bad Things.
Debra's grandfather may be good in other ways. But his abuse is wrong and must be stopped.

Rule #5, Abuse Will Not Stop by Itself.
Debra did the right thing when she told her teacher. When the social worker made grandpa move out, the abuse stopped.

Rule #6, Keep Telling People Until Someone Listens.
Debra was afraid to tell her mom or dad about the sexual abuse. When she told her teacher, her teacher asked her a lot of questions. But she believed Debra and called the social worker.

Rule #7, What Happens to the Sexual Abuser Is Never Your Fault.
After he left, grandpa didn't call for six months. Debra felt very sad about this. Finally, grandpa called. He told Debra he was sorry for what he had done and that it was his fault. He told Debra he loved her.

Chapter 5

Leota and Her Brother

Leota is almost nine. She lives with her mother and her seventeen-year-old brother, Alonzo. They live in a two-room apartment. She and Alonzo share a room. Sometimes her mother works at night. When this happens, Alonzo baby-sits. When Leota goes to bed, Alonzo stays up to watch television.

Leota's friends think Alonzo is a great dancer. Leota wishes Alonzo would pay attention to her. When she tries to get his attention, he tells her to shut up or go away.

The first time Alonzo bothered Leota in bed, she was almost asleep. She felt hands on her bottom. She thought it was her mother tucking her in. The next night she heard Alonzo cross the room. He sat

Sexual abuse can destroy the trust between a brother and sister.

on the edge of her bed. He put his hand in her pajamas. He felt around below her tummy. Then he went back to his bed. She lay awake and felt scared.

A week later her brother touched her again. This time she pretended to be asleep. He put his hand in her pajamas and started rubbing her genitals. When this happened she had a tingling feeling. She was also confused. She wanted Alonzo to like her. She knew that what he was doing was wrong. But she thought it was her fault.

Alonzo continued to sexually abuse Leota. When Alonzo rubbed her, neither of them spoke. Several times he even got under the covers with Leota. Then he rubbed his penis against her. She kept her eyes closed. Outside the bedroom Alonzo pretended Leota didn't exist.

Leota started to worry all the time. She felt different from her friends. She stayed by herself. She was sure everyone knew about her and Alonzo. She had trouble in school. She failed tests in spelling, her best subject.

One day Maria, a girl in Leota's class, asked what was wrong. Leota told her. Maria listened

Leota started to worry all the time. She felt different from her friends. She stayed by herself.

carefully. She didn't fully understand. But she
knew Alonzo was hurting Leota. The next day
Maria's mother called Leota's mother on the
phone. They talked for a long time.

That night Leota's mother stayed home from
work. She made Alonzo move his bed into the
living room. She moved her own bed into the room
with Leota. The next time she had to work at night
she called Carmen, Maria's older sister, to baby-sit
for Leota.

Leota's mother called a child worker. The child
worker made Alonzo go to a doctor about his
problem.

For several weeks Leota blushed whenever she
saw Alonzo. Then she felt okay. She and Maria
became best friends.

A year later, Alonzo told Leota he was sorry
about what he had done.

The Seven Rules about sexual abuse help us
understand Leota's story.

The most important lesson Leota learned was
Rule #2, Sexual Abuse Is Never Your Fault.

Leota knew that Alonzo liked to touch her. She
loved her brother. She wanted him to hug her and
love her back. She thought he would love her more
if she let him do what he wanted.

Children want and need affection. Sometimes
older people make it hard to get affection in good

Constant worrying may lead to depression.

ways. Children sometimes think they have to get it any way they can. But no matter how a child acts, she or he should not be abused.

Leota lay in her bed quietly when Alonzo touched her. Does that mean what happened was her fault? No. The victim of sexual abuse is never to blame. Children simply are not responsible for what an older, stronger person does.

Leota also learned Rule #1, Your Body Belongs to You.

Almost everyone likes to be hugged by a parent or caring adult. And sometimes we let a relative hug us when we don't want to. That kind of touching is okay.

When children are small they may play sexual games. This kind of touching is okay too. But when an adult or a person who is much older plays sexual games with a child, that is abuse.

Two young people about the same age who love or care for each other may touch sexually. That kind of touching is also okay.

When a person has no control over how, when, or where he or she is touched sexually, that is abuse.

Rule #3 applies too. Abuse Is Always Harmful.

Alonzo was gentle when he touched Leota. So that part didn't hurt. But Leota was hurt in other ways. She stayed by herself. She started to worry all the time. She did badly in spelling.

Rule #4 is Good People Do Bad Things.

Leota's friends thought Alonzo was neat. So did Leota. She wanted Alonzo to like her. When he

Sometimes older people make it hard to get affection in good ways.

touched her genitals she had a tingling feeling.
When that happened, she thought, "I am bad."
Leota learned that Alonzo was wrong, not she. She
learned that he could abuse her even though he
was her brother. When Alonzo got help with his
problem, he said he was sorry.

Rule #5 is Sexual Abuse Does Not Stop by
Itself.

Maria saw something was wrong. She asked to
help. This was very brave. But Maria could not
stop Alonzo. So she told her mother. When
Alonzo's mother found out, she called a child
worker. A child worker's job is to protect children
from abuse. Alonzo would not have stopped
bothering his sister if Maria had not told her
mother.

Rule #6 is Keep Telling People You Trust Until
Someone Listens.

Leota was lucky. Her friend cared enough to ask
what was wrong. Even if Maria didn't fully
understand, she knew what to do.

Rule #7 is What Happens to the Abuser Is
Never Your Fault.

Alonzo's bed was moved. He had to go for help.
All this was his fault, not Leota's. Still, Leota felt
sorry for Alonzo.

Abused children sometimes become bullies.

Chapter 6

What Happened to Billy?

Billy was eleven years old. A seven-year-old boy named Sam lived next door. Sam had a rabbit named Black Jack. Sam loved Black Jack very much.

One day the boys were alone in Billy's yard. Billy told Sam to follow him into the garage. "I have something special for you," Billy said. Billy closed the door. He unzipped his pants and took out his penis. He grabbed Sam by the neck and pushed him down.

"Put it in your mouth," he told Sam. "If you don't, I'll kill Black Jack." Sam did what Billy said.

Billy told Sam his father and mother would die if he told. "And I won't be your friend," Billy said. Sam was very scared. So he kept the secret.

Sam was in the first grade. At school he started hitting other children. The teacher asked Sam's parents if anything was wrong. She also asked Sam. But he kept quiet.

Things got worse. Sam started to wet his bed. He woke up in the night crying. His mother went to his bed. Sam said, "I don't want you to die, Mommy."

One day Sam was in the bathroom at school with another little boy. They had their pants down. Sam grabbed the boy. He pointed to his penis. "Take it in your mouth," he said. The boy knocked Sam down, and Sam cried. Then Sam told the teacher what Billy had made him do in the garage. The teacher was very upset. She told Sam's parents. She also called a child worker.

Sam's father yelled at Billy. Later he yelled at Billy's mother. Billy started to cry. He told his mother that a bigger boy had been making him do the same thing he made Sam do. The bigger boy was a bully. Billy was afraid of him, just as Sam was afraid of Billy.

The child worker went to Sam's house. First she talked to Sam, then to Billy. She also visited the bully and his family. The bully was sent for help.

The most important lesson to learn from this story is Rule #3, Sexual Abuse Is Always Harmful.

Sometimes children who are sexually abused will abuse other children who are weaker. Or they may hurt pets. When Billy was abused, he didn't know what to do. He was scared. But he was also angry. He felt that this should not have happened to a big boy like him. Maybe something was wrong with him, he thought. He felt bad about himself. He didn't want anyone to find out that he was weak. So he proved he was stronger than Sam. He abused his friend.

After that, Sam had bad feelings also. He had nightmares. He dreamed he was falling into blackness, alone and scared. Sometimes in his nightmare, a huge shape like a bowling ball was trying to crush him. When he awoke, he had wet his bed. There is another lesson here, too.

Rule #5 is Sexual Abuse Does Not Stop by Itself.

Children who are abused when they are very young may not even have the words to explain what happened to them. Sam knew what Billy had done was wrong. But he had no idea it was sexual abuse.

Sometimes we keep secrets because we think it will be fun. Or we keep secrets because we want to surprise someone. Surprise, which you will tell later to make someone happy, is a good idea. Secrets that you are never supposed to tell are a bad idea. The secret of sexual abuse keeps hurting until it is shared.

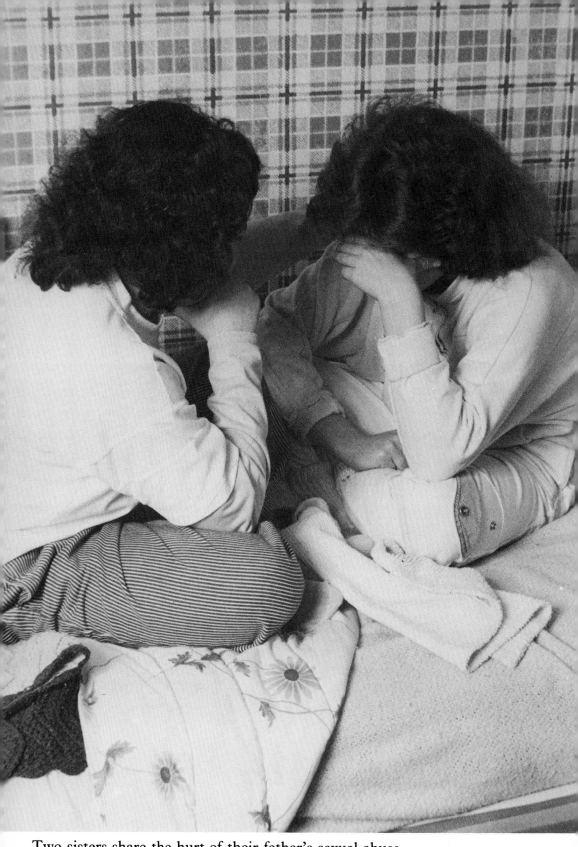

Two sisters share the hurt of their father's sexual abuse.

Chapter 7

The Problem of Incest

Roseann was twelve. She and her older sister, Doreen, lived in a small house with their father. Their parents were divorced.

Roseann felt that her father did not love her. He gave Doreen lots of special presents. But he hardly gave Roseann anything. When Doreen yelled at Roseann, their father always took Doreen's side.

Roseann's father often made her leave the house at night. He told her to go to a friend's house. Or he told her to just go outside.

One night Roseann came back early. She opened the door quietly. She heard her father and Doreen making noises in the bedroom. She had heard those noises when her father and mother had "private time." She had heard those noises on TV.

She knew they were the noises people made when they had intercourse.

She was very confused. The next day she asked Doreen what had happened. Doreen told her to shut up and mind her own business.

Another time Roseann came into the house and saw Doreen naked in her father's bedroom. Her father had gone out. When Roseann came into the bedroom, Doreen started to cry. Roseann put her arm around her older sister. She asked what was wrong.

Doreen said, "Daddy did something dirty to me." Roseann was scared. "I don't understand," she said.

Then Doreen told Roseann about incest. She said their father was having intercourse with her. Doreen said they had been having sex since their mother left, for about three years. Doreen explained that her father only wanted her to be with him and wouldn't let her even go out with friends. Then Doreen told Roseann she was moving out. When she said this, Roseann began crying. "Watch out or he'll do it to you," Doreen said. She hugged her little sister.

After Doreen moved out, Roseann was afraid of her father. At night she heard him walking around the house. When he wanted her to stay home, she found excuses to go out.

He grabbed her and threw her onto the couch...
He said he would hit her.
But she kept yelling for help.

One night Roseann was reading. Her father was drinking beer. He asked her to dance. Roseann was afraid. She said okay. Her father started to rub her in a sexual way. When the music stopped, he held her tight.

"Come on," he told her. He wanted her to go to his bedroom. "I'll show you what your sister liked," he said. Roseann screamed and hit her father with her fists. When he let go she ran out of the house.

Roseann went to her aunt's house. She told her aunt what happened. Her aunt didn't believe Roseann and got angry. Then she called her father. Her father took her back home. He told her if she told anyone again, he would kill her.

Several weeks later Roseann's father was drunk. He grabbed her and threw her onto a couch. He tore her clothes. She started to scream again. He said he would hit her. But she kept yelling for help.

A neighbor called the police. When the police
came, Roseann's father went to the door. He told
the police everything was all right. But Roseann
told the police what had happened. She showed
them her torn clothes. They put handcuffs on her
father and took him to jail. Later Roseann talked to
a police officer who works with children. She told
the police officer that her father had intercourse
with her sister Doreen. The police officer saw that
Roseann understood this was incest. Doreen also
talked to the police officer.

The police officer called Roseann's aunt. She
helped Roseann's aunt understand what had
happened. Roseann went to live with her aunt.

The most important rule in this story is
Rule #6, Keep Telling People About Sexual Abuse
Until Someone Listens.

Sometimes, adults don't believe children who
talk about sexual abuse. Sometimes they even get
angry, like Roseann's aunt. It is very hard for an
adult to believe someone in their family could
commit sexual abuse.

Roseann didn't tell anyone else because she was
scared. Her father said he would kill her. But the
next time he abused her, she screamed so much a
neighbor called the police. Even though the police
asked her a lot of questions, she made them believe
her. Incest is a crime. So Roseann's father was
arrested.

Roseann also learned other things about sexual abuse. Rule #1 is Your Body Belongs to You.

Roseann wanted her father to love her. He gave presents to Doreen, but not to her. Roseann was jealous. But when Doreen explained incest to Roseann, she felt sorry for Doreen. When her father tried to abuse her, she knew this was not a good way to get love.

Rule #2 is Sexual Abuse Is Never Your Fault.

Doreen loved her younger sister Roseann. She didn't want their father to have sex with Roseann. Doreen did not know how to protect her sister. She moved out of the house to protect herself.

Roseann's father was lonely when his wife left. He started to have sex with Doreen. He gave her presents for sex. Doreen and her father had intercourse many times. But Doreen is not responsible for what her father did to her. And she is not responsible for what her father tried to do with Roseann. Only her father was responsible.

Rule #3 is Sexual Abuse Is Always Harmful.

Doreen was not hurt physically by their father. He wanted her to replace his wife. So he gave her presents. But she still hurt deep inside. Doreen had very few friends. When she started to date, she thought "no one will care for me unless I have sex with them." At first she was angry when Roseann asked what was happening. The next time, she cried. Then she moved out of the house.

Victims of incest may get angry at people around them for not protecting them. Doreen was angry at Roseann even though Roseann was younger. Both daughters might have been angry at their mother for leaving and not protecting them from incest.

Rule #4 is Good People Do Bad Things.

Roseann loved her father. She trusted him. She also loved and trusted Doreen. At first she could not believe what she heard or what she saw. When Doreen cried, Roseann saw she was being hurt by their father. She understood that someone you trust can commit the crime of incest.

Rule #5 is also important in this story. Sexual Abuse Doesn't Stop by Itself.

Roseann's sister left home. Then their father wanted to have sex with Roseann.

When Roseann's father abused her the first time, she ran out of the house. He promised not to bother her again. But he did. When that happened, she told the police. They were able to stop her father from attacking her again.

Rule #7 is What Happens to a Sexual Abuser Is Never Your Fault.

Roseann was sorry that her father went to jail. But she knew it was his fault, not hers. If he had not abused her—and her sister—he would not have gone to jail.

Chapter 8

The Crime of Rape

When Debra was sexually abused by her grandfather, she told her teacher, Mrs. Markle. Then, Mrs. Markle called the child protection service. She also called Debra's mom. Debra's mom was mad that Debra hadn't told her about the abuse. But she understood that Debra was afraid Grandpa would have to leave.

Debra was lucky because her mom knew what to do. This is a story about a girl who was not so lucky.

When Rosa was 11, her father died of a heart attack. She lived with her mother and little six-year old brother, Juanito. A young friend of Rosa's father named Julio lived in her building.

Julio quit school when he was sixteen. Now, he did odd jobs, played cards with his friends and just hung out on the street.

A father has to listen to his child and try to understand what the child is feeling.

One day, when 11-year-old Rosa was coming home from school, Julio was rapping with his friends. He showed her a bracelet he had in his pocket and asked if she liked it. When she said yes, he gave it to her. He winked at his pals. The next day, he bought Rosa a soda. Then, a week later, she saw him again. He told her to follow him. He smiled like he had a secret place he wanted to show her. She was scared, but a little excited too. She felt really grown up. She liked the attention she was getting from Julio. She thought something special might happen.

Julio led Rosa down to the basement of a nearby building. "You wanna be my girl?" he asked her.

Rosa didn't know what to say. She was nervous. So she just stared. Before she knew what was happening, Julio was holding her and rubbing up against her. Then he let go. "You like that?" he asked. "I bet you never felt a man."

Rosa turned and wanted to run. But Julio jumped in front of her. He was still smiling. "Come on," he said. "We're going to have some fun." Then he pushed her into a small room with a mattress on the floor.

Rosa tried to resist. But Julio was too strong. He forced her to have sex. Then, he put a dollar in her pocket. He said that if she told anyone, he would kill her little brother. She was very frightened for Juanito's safety. He was so helpless!

Rosa was also afraid that her mother would find out what happened. She had told her that girls who had sex before they were married went to hell.

Julio took Rosa to the basement many times after that. If she didn't fight and just let him do what he wanted, he promised not to hurt Juanito. She hated his smell and felt awful when it was over, down in her stomach. But she was scared to tell anyone.

One day, Mrs. Sanchez saw Julio and Rosa in the basement. She guessed what was going on and called Rosa's Mom.

Mom: (on the phone) I can't believe this. You sure it was her?
Rosa: What's wrong Mom?
Mom: That was Mrs. Sanchez. She told me what you're doing with that guy Julio. God is going to punish you for this.
Rosa: (scared) What are you talking about? I didn't do anything.
Mom: You lie to me? I'll teach you to lie, you little puta! How much did he pay you?

Now, Rosa was confused. She had taken money. But only because Julio made her. Then, Rosa's mom slapped her. She started to cry.
Rosa: (crying) Mom, he hurt me and said he would kill Juanito. I couldn't stop him. I don't like him. I hate what he does. Help me, Mom. I'm so scared. I don't know what to do.

Mom: How could he make you do that if you don't want to? What do you think will happen now? No one will want you. You'll never get married. Mrs. Sanchez will tell everyone in the neighborhood. Everyone will

The sexual abuser often feels alone and separated from the people around him.

laugh at me. I'm going to find Julio and scratch his eyes out and then I'll deal with you.

Rosa's mother ran out the door. Rosa was scared about what she might do. She just sat and cried.

The next day, Rosa heard what happened. Her mom and Julio got into a violent argument and the police had to be called to break it up. They had to go to the police station. When Rosa's mom finally got home she was afraid to talk about what had happened. Rosa wanted to run away from home.

Later that summer, Rosa's aunt came to visit from Puerto Rico. When she heard what happened, she called Rosa aside.

"Rosa," she said, "you were raped." Rosa had heard the word before and knew rape was a terrible thing. But she had not thought this was what happened to her. She thought rape was only by strangers.

"When I was a girl, I was raped too," said Rosa's aunt. "Whenever someone makes you have sex against your will, that is rape," she said. "You weren't bad. What Julio did was a terrible crime and he should be punished. You feel guilty because you took money and because your mother got into trouble with the police. But you took money because you were scared and didn't know what to do.

"This Julio has a serious problem," Rosa's aunt explained. "You made a mistake and got tricked. But adults are stronger and bigger than kids. That's why kids need help when adults force them to do something they don't want to do. Lots of kids make mistakes worse than the one you made."

Rosa asked her aunt, "What should I do now?"
"We're going to call the police. Then you and I are going to explain to them what happened. Then I will talk to your mother.
Rosa was worried. "What will they do to Julio?"

"They'll punish him and then they'll get him help so he doesn't trick or hurt any more girls. You know, Rosa, if he did this to you, he probably did it to other girls before. We're going to stop him. You and me. Okay?"

Rosa wasn't sure, but she said okay.

Rape

Julio forced Rosa to have sex against her will. This form of sexual abuse is called rape. When we think of rape we think of strangers. Rosa knew Julio. Most rapes are committed by people who know their victims. Remember Rule #1, Your Body Belongs to You. No one has the right to make you have sex when you don't want it. Rape is a very serious crime.

Rosa's Mother

When Rosa told her mother about her sexual abuse, she could only think about herself and her family's pride. Her first thought was how to hurt Julio, not how to protect and help Rosa.

What should Rosa's mother have done?

First, she could have told her about rape. Then, she could have explained Rule #2, Abuse is Never Your Fault. This would have been very hard for her to do.

Teenagers want to be liked by adults. But no one has to allow unwanted touching.

Rosa's mother loves her. So she got mad when Rosa was hurt. But even if she took money, Julio was the one who was wrong, not Rosa. After she got mad, she should have listened to Rosa more closely. She should have tried to figure out what she was feeling.

Children want and need caring from the adults around them. They may try adult behavior to get attention. Rosa liked getting attention from Julio and his friends. So when he asked her to follow him, she was confused about what to do. But no matter what a child does, they should not be abused.

What to do?

When Debra was sexually abused, her teacher called child protection services. Then, child protection services sent a social worker to talk to Debra's grandfather. The social worker told her grandfather he would have to move out of their house and get a place of his own.

Debra's teacher could call child protection because she was abused by her grandfather, a member of her family. Child protective services only deal with abuse when it is by a family member. When someone is abused by a person who is not related to them, they should call the police. Rosa's aunt was right.

What happened next?

The day after Rosa talked to the police, everyone at school was talking about her and Julio. Julio's sister told Rosa she would get her after school. Julio's friends made fun of Rosa.

But then Laura Sanchez came up to Rosa. Laura was
the daughter of the woman who had seen Rosa and
Julio in the basement. Laura told Rosa that Julio had
done the same thing to her. The two girls held each
other and cried. Then, Laura told the police
everything.

Julio went on trial. At the trial Rosa and Laura told
their stories. Rosa's aunt came to court too. So did a
police woman who works with victims of rape and
sexual abuse.

Rosa was first questioned by her lawyer who was
very kind. Then Julio's lawyer got up. He tried to show
that Rosa was lying. That what she said never
happened. Then he tried to show that because she took
money it was her fault. Rosa thought about what her
aunt had told her. Even though it was hard, she told
the truth because she didn't want Julio to hurt other
girls.

Julio was sent to jail. In jail he got therapy. Each
week, he went to a group with other men who had
abused or raped girls. Rosa graduated from high
school and was working at a store in the neighborhood.
Julio got out of jail after 2 years and moved back home.
But he never bothered Rosa, Laura or any other girls in
the neighborhood. Today, Rosa and Laura are still
friends.

Chapter 9

Stopping Sexual Abuse

Stopping abuse is not easy.

Boys who are abused may think that talking about abuse means they are not brave. They may think if they are afraid of sexual abuse they are not real men. Or they may think that being sexually abused means they are homosexuals. Girls who are abused may think they can never marry or have healthy children. They may be afraid of making close friends. They may think the only way to get love is with sex. None of these things is true.

It is normal to be afraid when someone who is older or stronger than you are abuses you.

Sexual abuse can hurt you in many ways. But it will not make you into a homosexual. And it will not keep you from getting married or being a good parent. Most children who are abused grow up to have happy sex lives.

It was hard for Debra, Leota, Rosa, Roseann, Sam, and Billy to tell their stories. Talking about sexual abuse is brave. By making their problems known, the children in this book helped prevent others from being abused.

Some adults will not listen to children who talk about abuse. Some think it is bad for children to talk about sex. But remember all the people who do listen. Remember Debra's teacher and Leota's friend, Maria. Remember the police officer who helped Roseann, the teacher who listened to Sam, and the child worker who helped Sam and Billy. And remember how Rosa and her aunt worked together to stop abuse.

There is no one way to stop abuse. Each person will deal with it in his or her own way.

Sexual abuse is the secret that is now being shared. And when it is shared, it can be stopped.

Glossary — *Explaining New Words*

abuser Someone you know and trust who tries to hurt you sexually.

genitals These are sexual organs. Examples of genitals are a boy's penis and a girl's vagina.

incest Sexual intercourse between people who are closely related by blood.

intercourse When the male penis is placed inside the vagina of a female.

molester A stranger or someone you barely know who tries to hurt you sexually.

privacy The right to be left alone.

rape When one person forces another person to have sexual relations.

survivor Someone who was hurt or abused in the past.

victim Someone who is being hurt or abused.

Where To Go for Help

LOCAL RESOURCES:

School personnel, including teachers, counselors, social workers, psychologists, nurses, and administrators

Police officers

Librarians

Members of the clergy

Medical personnel

Rape crisis center staff members

Crisis intervention centers

YWCAs

YMCAs

CHILD WELFARE
LEAGUE OF AMERICA
440 1st Street, NW
Washington, DC 20001
(202) 638-2952

CHILDHELP USA
6463 Independence Avenue
Woodland Hills, CA 91367
Hotline: 1-800-4-A-CHILD
or 1-800-422-4453

NATIONAL
COMMITTEE FOR
PREVENTION OF
CHILD ABUSE
332 South Michigan
Avenue
Chicago, IL 60604
(312) 663-3520

For Further Reading

Aho, Jennifer Bowle and John W. Petras. *Learning About Sexual Abuse*. New York: Enslow Publications, Inc., 1985, 86 pages. (Grades 5–8) This book explains sexual abuse, what to do if it happens to you, and how to avoid it.

Hyde, Margaret O. *Sexual Abuse—Let's Talk About It*. PA: Westminster Press, 1984, 93 pages. This book discusses the sexual abuse of children, how they can protect themselves, and how to get help.

Terkel, Susan Neiburg and Janice E. Rench. *Feeling Safe, Feeling Strong: How to Avoid Sexual Abuse and What to Do if It Happens to You*. Minneapolis, MN: Lerner Publications Co., 1984, 68 pages. This book describes instances of different kinds of sexual abuse.

Index

About the Author
Evan Stark is a well-known sociologist, educator, and therapist as well as a popular lecturer on women's and children's health issues. Dr. Stark was the Henry Rutgers Fellow at Rutgers University, an associate at the Institution for Social and Policy Studies at Yale University, and a Fulbright Fellow at the University of Essex. He is the author of many publications in the field of family relations and is the father of four children.

Acknowledgments and Photo Credits

P. 20, Blackbirch Graphics, Inc.; all other photos, Stuart Rabinowitz.

Design/Production: Blackbirch Graphics, Inc.
Cover Photograph: Stuart Rabinowitz